10 REASONS JESUS CAME TO DIE

JOHN PIPER

*Why did Jesus Christ suffer and die?
I believe that is the most important question
of the twenty-first century. Here are ten
answers from the Bible.*

JESUS CAME TO DIE...

#10) TO DESTROY HOSTILITY BETWEEN RACES

The suspicion, prejudice, and demeaning attitudes between Jews and non-Jews in Bible times were as serious as the racial, ethnic, and national hostilities today. Jesus died to create a whole new way for races to be reconciled: he "has broken down…the dividing wall of hostility…making peace…through the cross" (Ephesians 2:14-16).

It is impossible to build lasting unity among races by saying that all religions can come together as equally valid. God sent his Son into the world as the only means of saving sinners and reconciling races. Only as the races find this reconciliation will they love and enjoy each other.

blood and righteousness of Christ credited to our account.

#6) TO RECONCILE US TO GOD

The reconciliation that needs to happen between man and God goes both ways. God's first act in reconciling us to himself was to remove the obstacle that separated him from us—the guilt of our sin. He took the steps we could not take to remove his own judgment by sending Jesus to suffer in our place: "While we were enemies we were reconciled to God by the death of his Son" (Romans 5:10). Reconciliation from our side is simply to receive what God has already done, the way we receive an infinitely valuable gift.

#5) TO SHOW GOD'S LOVE FOR SINNERS

The measure of God's love is shown by the degree of his sacrifice in saving us from the penalty of our sins: "he gave his only Son" (John 3:16). When we add the horrific crucifixion that Christ endured, it becomes clear that the sacrifice the Father and the Son made to save us was indescribably great!

The measure of his love increases still more when we consider the degree of our unworthiness. "God shows his love for us in that while we were still sinners, Christ died for us" (Romans 5:8). Our debt is so great, only a divine sacrifice could pay it.

#4) TO SHOW JESUS' OWN LOVE FOR US

The death of Christ is also the supreme expression that he "loved me and gave himself for me" (Galatians 2:20). It is my sin that cuts me off from God. All I can do is plead for mercy.

I see Christ suffering and dying "to give his life as a ransom for many" (Matthew 20:28). And I ask, am I among the "many"? And I hear the answer, "Whoever believes in him should not perish but have eternal life" (John 3:16). Jesus paid the highest price possible to give me—personally—the greatest gift possible.

#3) TO TAKE AWAY OUR CONDEMNATION

The great conclusion to the suffering and death of Christ is this: "There is therefore now no condemnation for those who are in Christ Jesus" (Romans 8:1). To be "in Christ" means to be in relationship to him by faith. Christ becomes our punishment (which we don't have to bear) and our worth before God (which we cannot earn). The death of Christ secures freedom from condemnation for those who believe that Christ has served their death sentence. It is as sure that they cannot be condemned as it is sure that Christ died!

#2) TO BRING US TO GOD

"Gospel" means "good news," and it all ends in one thing: God himself. The gospel is the good news that at the cost of his Son's life, God has done everything necessary to captivate us with what will make us eternally and ever-increasingly happy—namely, himself. "Christ… suffered once for sins, the righteous for the unrighteous, that he might bring us to God" (1 Peter 3:18).

#1) TO GIVE ETERNAL LIFE TO ALL WHO BELIEVE ON HIM

Jesus made it plain that rejecting the eternal life he offered would result in the misery of eternity in hell: "Whoever does not believe is condemned already….the wrath of God remains on him" (John 3:18, 36).

But for those who trust Christ, the best is yet

to come. "No eye has seen, nor ear heard, nor the heart of man imagined what God has prepared for those who love him" (1 Corinthians 2:9). We will see the all-satisfying glory of God. "This is eternal life, that they know you the only true God, and Jesus Christ whom you have sent" (John 17:3).

For all these reasons and more, Christ suffered and died. Why would you not embrace him as your Savior from sin and judgment, and live with God eternally?

If you are moved to embrace God's Son in this way, tell God in words like these:

Dear God, I'm convinced that Jesus suffered and died for my sins. I gratefully trust in him now as my Lord and my precious Treasure and the only way I'll ever receive your forgiveness and your promise of eternal life. Amen.

CROSSWAY | Good News Tracts

ISBN 978-1-68216-002-2

www.goodnewstracts.org